8.04

Drawing
and Learning About
Dinosaurs

Using Shapes
and Lines

by
Amy Bailey Muehlenhardt

Thanks to our advisers for their expertise, research, and advice:

Peter Dodson, Ph.D.
Professor of Veterinary Gross Anatomy
Professor of Earth and Environmental Sciences
University of Pennsylvania
Philadelphia, Pennsylvania

Susan Kesselring, M.A., Literacy Educator
Rosemount-Apple Valley-Eagan (Minnesota) School District

PICTURE WINDOW BOOKS
Minneapolis, Minnesota

Amy Bailey Muehlenhardt
grew up in Fergus Falls, Minnesota,
and attended Minnesota State
University in Moorhead. She holds
a Bachelor of Science degree in
Graphic Design and Art Education.
Before coming to Picture Window
Books, Amy was an elementary art
teacher. She always impressed upon
her students that "everyone is an artist."
Amy lives in Mankato, Minnesota,
with her husband, Brad.

To Craig and Brad—you both are
wonderful husbands and fathers.
To my Waconia students—every time you solve
a problem, you are thinking like an artist.
Be creative, and keep drawing!

ABM

Managing Editor: Bob Temple
Creative Director: Terri Foley
Editor: Sara E. Hoffmann
Editorial Adviser: Andrea Cascardi
Designer: Amy Bailey Muehlenhardt
Page production: Picture Window Books
The illustrations in this book were drawn with pencil.

Picture Window Books
5115 Excelsior Boulevard
Suite 232
Minneapolis, MN 55416
1-877-845-8392
www.picturewindowbooks.com

Printed in the United States of America.

Library of Congress Cataloging-in-Publication Data
Muehlenhardt, Amy Bailey, 1974-
Drawing and learning about dinosaurs : using shapes and lines/
by Amy Bailey Muehlenhardt
p. cm — (Sketch it!)
Summary: Provides step-by-step instructions for drawing
various types of dinosaurs, using circles, squares,
triangles, and other simple shapes.
Includes bibliographical references.
ISBN 1-4048-0268-1 (Reinforced Library Binding)
1. Dinosaurs in art—Juvenile literature.
2. Drawing—Technique—Juvenile literature. [1. Dinosaurs
in art. 2. Drawing—Technique.] I. Title.
NC780.5 .M84 2004
743.6'79—dc22

2003018492

Table of Contents

Everyone Is an Artist

There is no right or wrong way to draw!

With a little patience and some practice, anyone can learn to draw. Did you know every picture begins as a simple shape? If you can draw shapes, you can draw anything.

The Basics of Drawing

line—a long mark made by a pen, a pencil, or another tool

guideline—a line used to help you draw. The guideline will be erased when your drawing is almost complete.

shade—to color in with your pencil

value—the lightness or darkness of an object

shape—the form or outline of an object or figure

diagonal—a shape or line that leans to the side

Before you begin, you will need:

a pencil
an eraser
lots of paper

Four Tips for Drawing

1. Draw very lightly.
To see how this is done, try drawing soft, medium, and dark lines. The softer you press, the lighter the lines will be.

2. Draw your shapes.
Connect them with a dark, sketchy line.

3. Add details.
Details are small things that make a good picture even better.

4. Smudge your art.
Use your finger to rub your lines. This will soften your picture and add shadows.

Let's get started!

Simple shapes help you draw.

Practice drawing these shapes before you begin:

○ **circle**
A circle is round like a bouncing ball.

△ **triangle**
A triangle has three sides and three corners.

⬭ **oval**
An oval is a circle with its cheeks sucked in.

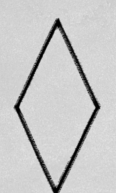 **diamond**
A diamond is two triangles put together.

◠ **arc**
An arc is half of a circle. It looks like a turtle's shell.

□ **square**
A square has four equal sides and four corners.

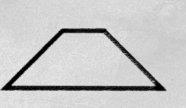 **trapezoid**
A trapezoid has four sides and four corners. Two of its sides are different lengths.

 **crescent**
A crescent looks like a banana.

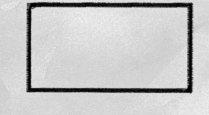 **rectangle**
A rectangle has two long sides, two short sides, and four corners.

You will also use lines when drawing.

Practice drawing these lines:

vertical
A vertical line stands tall like a tree.

zig zag
A zig-zag line is sharp and pointy.

horizontal
A horizontal line lies down and takes a nap.

wavy
A wavy line moves up and down like a roller coaster.

diagonal
A diagonal line leans to the side.

Remember to practice drawing.

While using this book, you may want to stop drawing at step five or six. That's great! Everyone is at a different drawing level.

dizzy
A dizzy line spins around and around.

Don't worry if your picture isn't perfect. The important thing is to have fun. You may wish to add details to your drawing. Does your dinosaur live near water? What color is your dinosaur? Create a background.

Be creative!

Compsognathus (KOMP-sog-NAY-thus)

Compsognathus was one of the smallest dinosaurs. It looked
a little like a bird, but it had a lizard-like tail. Compsognathus
had three-toed feet. It ate insects and small lizards.

Step 1

Draw an oval for the body. Draw a
circle for the head.

Step 2

Connect the circle and the oval with
two curved lines for the neck.

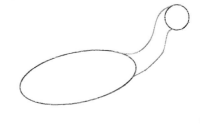

Step 3

Draw a circle for an eye. Add two
triangles for the beak. Draw a
zig-zag line for sharp teeth. Add a
long crescent for the tail.

Step 4

Draw a large oval for the back
thigh. Add an oval and two
rectangles for the shin and foot.
Draw one triangle claw. Draw a
square and a rectangle for the other
shin and foot. Draw three triangles
for claws.

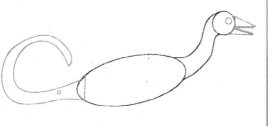

Step 5

Draw two smaller ovals for the front upper arms. Add two squares and two rectangles for forearms. Add four triangles for the claws.

Step 6

Draw a darker, sketchy line around the shapes. Erase the lines you no longer want. Begin adding oval spots on the back.

Step 7

Compsognathus was darker on its back than on its tummy. Shade in the oval spots with your pencil. Shade around the eye. It will look as if Compsognathus is wearing a mask.

Diplodocus (die-PLOH-dah-kus)

Diplodocus was a giant dinosaur. It was as long as two school buses put together! Diplodocus had nostrils on top of its head and had very weak teeth. It was a plant-eater.

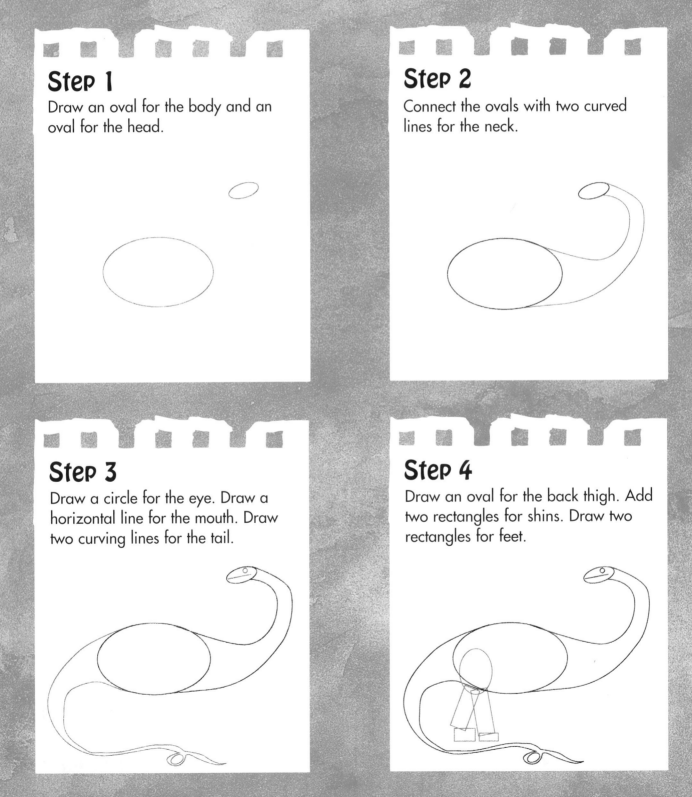

Step 1
Draw an oval for the body and an oval for the head.

Step 2
Connect the ovals with two curved lines for the neck.

Step 3
Draw a circle for the eye. Draw a horizontal line for the mouth. Draw two curving lines for the tail.

Step 4
Draw an oval for the back thigh. Add two rectangles for shins. Draw two rectangles for feet.

Step 5

Draw an oval for the front thigh. Add two rectangles for shins. Draw two rectangles for feet. Add two triangles for claws.

Step 6

Draw a darker, sketchy line around the shapes. Erase the lines you no longer want. Begin adding wavy lines for the tough skin.

Step 7

Shade in with the side of your pencil. Diplodocus had thick, tough skin, so use a lot of wavy lines.

Pachycephalosaurus (PACK-ee-cef-AH-loh-SORE-us)

Pachycephalosaurus had a huge, dome-shaped head. Its head was covered with spikes. It had two powerful back legs used for running and walking. Pachycephalosaurus had short arms. It was a plant-eater.

Step 1
Draw an oval for the body. Draw an oval for the head. Draw a circle for the eye. Add two arcs for the beak. The top arc is larger than the bottom arc.

Step 2
Connect the ovals with two curved lines for the neck. Pachycephalosaurus had bumps all over its head. Draw circles and ovals for the bumps.

Step 3
Draw a large oval for the thigh and an oval for the shin. Draw an oval for the other thigh.

Step 4
Draw two rectangles for shins. On the near side, draw another rectangle. Draw two triangles on each side to make feet.

Step 5

Draw an oval for the upper arm.
Draw two rectangles for the forearms.
Add zig-zag lines for claws. Draw a
triangle tail.

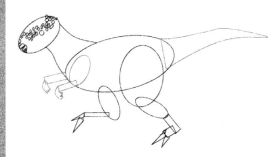

Step 6

Draw a darker, sketchy line around
the shapes. Erase the lines you no
longer want. Begin shading darker
spots on the back.

Step 7

Continue shading the spots. Shade in the eye and the
bumps on the head.

Spinosaurus (SPIE-noh-SORE-us)

Spinosaurus is called *spiny lizard* because it had large spines on its back. The spines could reach up to six feet (two meters) tall. Spinosaurus was a meat-eater. It had a powerful jaw with sharp teeth like a crocodile's.

Step 1

Draw two circles side by side for the body. One circle should be larger than the other. Add a circle for the head.

Step 2

Connect the three circles with curving lines for the neck and body. Draw two rectangles for the snout. Draw a small circle for the eye.

Step 3

Draw two ovals for the upper arms. Draw two rectangles for the forearms. Add zig-zag lines for the claws.

Step 4

Draw a large oval for the thigh. Draw an oval for the knee. Add two rectangles for the shin and foot. Draw a zig-zag line for the claws. Add a triangle tail.

14

Step 5

Draw an oval for the other thigh.
Add an oval for the knee and two
rectangles for the shin and foot. Add
a zig-zag line for claws. Draw an
arc for the spine.

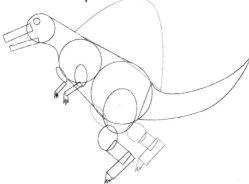

Step 6

Add a zig-zag line for sharp teeth.
Draw a darker, sketchy line around
the shapes. Erase the lines you no
longer want.

Step 7

Add long triangles inside the spine. Shade them in
with your pencil. Add small circles for scales.

Stegosaurus (STEG-oh-SORE-us)

Stegosaurus's back legs were longer than its front legs. It had diamond-shaped plates on its back and spikes on its tail. Stegosaurus was a plant-eater.

Step 1
Draw an oval for the body. The oval should be tilted higher in the back. Draw an oval for the head.

Step 2
Connect the head and the body with two curving lines for the neck. Draw a circle for the eye. Add two small triangles for the beak.

Step 3
Draw two ovals for the arms. Add two rectangles for the shins.

Step 4
Draw two ovals for the thighs. Draw two rectangles for the shins. Add a triangle tail.

Step 5

Draw small diamonds on top of the neck. Draw larger diamonds on the back. The diamonds should get smaller again as you draw farther down the tail. Add three triangles on the tail.

Step 6

Draw a darker, sketchy line around the shapes. Erase the lines you no longer want. When tracing, begin rounding the points of the diamonds. Add small arcs on the feet for claws.

Step 7

Shade in the Stegosaurus with the side of your pencil. Darken the eye. Add dark and light shadows on the spikes.

Triceratops (trie-SAIR-ah-TOPS)

Triceratops looked a little like a rhinoceros. It had three horns and a beak. Triceratops looked fierce—but it ate plants instead of other animals.

Step 1

Draw an oval for the body. Draw an oval for the head.

Step 2

Draw an arc for the eye. Add two triangles for the beak. Connect the beak to the head with two short lines. Connect the head and the body with two curving lines for the neck.

Step 3

Add a triangle between the head and the body. The triangle is the crest. Draw two ovals for the thigh and the arm.

Step 4

Add four rectangles for the shins. Draw four circles for the feet.

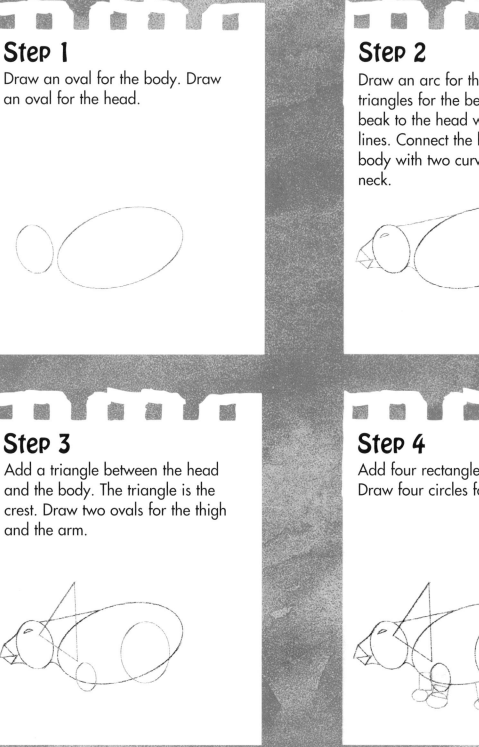

Step 5

Draw three triangles for horns on Triceratops's head. Two horns are long and slender triangles. The third horn is a smaller triangle. Draw a triangle for the tail. Add a curved line for the mouth.

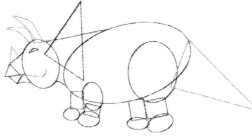

Step 6

Draw a darker, sketchy line around the shapes. Draw a wavy line along the back of the crest. Erase the lines you no longer want. Begin shading the crest with diagonal lines.

Step 7

Continue shading. The crest has darker shadows because it is bumpy. Add wavy lines around the mouth. Add lines around the eye and shade it darker.

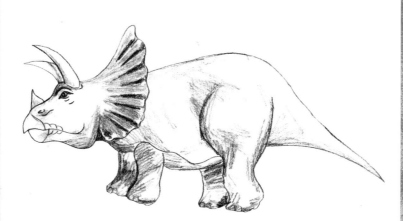

Tyrannosaurus rex (tie-RAN-oh-SORE-us REX)

Tyrannosaurus rex was one of the largest two-legged dinosaurs. It had a massive, powerful jaw with very large teeth. It had two strong back legs and two small arms. T. rex was so heavy, it could only run for a short distance.

Step 1

Draw an oval for the body. Draw a circle for the head.

Step 2

Connect the head and the body with two curved lines for the neck. Add a circle for the eye. Draw two rectangles and one triangle for the powerful jaws. Add a zig-zag line for large, sharp teeth.

Step 3

Draw an oval for the arm. Add two rectangles to the oval. Draw zig-zag lines for claws.

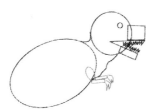

Step 4

Draw an oval for the thigh. Add a smaller oval for the shin. Draw a rectangle for the foot.

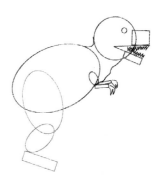

20

Step 5

Draw an oval for the other thigh. Add an oval for the shin. Draw a rectangle for the foot. Add a triangle tail.

Step 6

Draw a darker, sketchy line around the shapes. Erase the lines you no longer want. Begin adding curved lines for T. rex's rough skin.

Step 7

Shade in with the side of your pencil. Darken the eye and add curved lines around the eye.

Velociraptor  (vel-OS-ih-RAP-tore)

This fast-running dinosaur was a meat-eater. It was only six feet (two meters) long. Velociraptor had a long snout and very sharp teeth. Some people believe this dinosaur was very intelligent.

Step 1

Draw a circle for the body. Draw an oval for the head. Draw two triangles for the jaws.

Step 2

Connect the circle and the oval with two curved lines for the neck. Draw an arc for the eye. Add a diagonal line for the jaw.

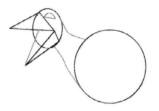

Step 3

Draw two ovals for the arms. Add two rectangles for the forearms. Draw two circles for the hands. Add zig-zag lines for the claws.

Step 4

Draw two ovals for thighs. Draw two rectangles for shins. Draw two rectangles for feet. On the near side, draw a small square for the toe. Draw three triangles for claws on each foot.

Step 5

Draw three zig-zag lines for teeth. Add a triangle tail.

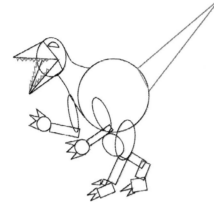

Step 6

Draw a darker, sketchy line around the shapes. Erase the lines you no longer want. Begin shading a zig-zag pattern on the back.

Step 7

Continue shading in the zig-zag pattern. Shade in the mouth, eye, and claws. On the far side, add a triangle for another claw on the foot.

To Learn More

At the Library

Dahl, Michael. *Swift Thief: The Adventure of Velociraptor.* Minneapolis: Picture Window Books, 2004.

Grambling, Lois G. *Can I Have a Stegosaurus, Mom? Can I? Please!?* Mahwah, N.J.: Bridge Water Books, 1995.

Heins, Edward. *Drawing Dinosaurs.* New York: Grosset & Dunlap, 2001.

Levin, Freddie. *1-2-3 Draw Dinosaurs and Other Prehistoric Animals.* Columbus, N.C.: Peel Productions, 2000.

Roberts, Michelle. *How to Draw Dinosaurs.* New York: Dover, 1995.

On the Web

Fact Hound

Fact Hound offers a safe, fun way to find Web sites related to this book. All of the sites on Fact Hound have been researched by our staff.
http://www.facthound.com

1. Visit the Fact Hound home page.
2. Enter a search word related to this book, or type in this special code: 1404802681.
3. Click on the FETCH IT button.

Your trusty Fact Hound will fetch the best sites for you!